# DELIGHT IN

## Margaret Barham

ARTHUR H. STOCKWELL LTD.
Elms Court   Ilfracombe   Devon
*Established 1898*

© *Margaret Barham, 1997*
*First published in Great Britain, 1997*

*All rights reserved.
No part of this publication may be reproduced
or transmitted in any form or by any means,
electronic or mechanical, including photocopy,
recording, or any information storage and
retrieval system, without permission
in writing from the copyright holder.*

*British Library Cataloguing-in-Publication Data.
A catalogue record for this book is available
from the British Library.*

By the same author:
*Hope in God*

ISBN 0 7223 3059-6

*Printed in Great Britain by
Arthur H. Stockwell Ltd.
Elms Court    Ilfracombe
Devon*

Scripture taken from the HOLY BIBLE, NEW INTERNATIONAL VERSION®. NIV® Copyright© 1973, 1978, 1984 by International Bible Society. Used by permission of International Bible Society. All rights reserved.

*But his delight is in the law of the LORD, and on his law he meditates day and night. Ps 1:2.*

As I was thinking about Psalm 1, I had the following thoughts:— Happy is the person who delights in reading the Bible, who spends time thinking about God's Word and putting it into practice. He does not take notice of those who tell him he is wasting his time and that he should be out enjoying himself and "living it up". No. He would rather spend time with God and His Word. He is like a tree — firm and sure. He is not rushing around trying to make a good impression. He is not trying to convince himself and others that he is a good Christian. He is in the place where God has planted him and he is bearing fruit for God. He does not have to prove to others or himself that he is fruitful. Anyone looking at him can see the life of Jesus shining out of him. When trouble comes, he does not shrivel up or give way under it — his leaves remain green. His roots go deep into God's Word, so that he has an abundant source to draw upon when the winds of adversity hit him. He still bears his Christian witness with joy, even in the most adverse circumstances. All this is possible because he delights in the law of the LORD.

May we have such a desire for God and His Word, that these things may be true of us.

*Ask of me, and I will make the nations your inheritance, the ends of the earth your possession. Ps 2:8.*

God our Father says to us, "Ask of Me." He says to us today, "Ask of Me, and I will give you every spiritual blessing in Jesus. Ask of Me, and you will possess all that you need to live the fulness of life that Jesus promised. Ask of Me, and I will give you power to control your unruly feelings and to overcome your self-will. Ask of Me, and I will give you the assurance that you are My child and that I am your Father, who knows all about your needs even before you ask, but I still desire that you should ask."

So often we do not have the wonderful blessings God wishes to give us simply because we do not ask. At other times we ask and do not receive because we ask with wrong motives or for our own self-gratification. God wants us to ask as children coming to a father. He desires to answer us in order that others may see His greatness, His abundance and His power to supply every need of His children.

God says to us now, "Ask of Me." May our times of asking also be times of delighting in the Lord.

*You have filled my heart with greater joy than when their grain and new wine abound.  Ps 4:7.*

There is joy at harvest when the crops are plentiful but it is a joy that fades as the barns begin to empty again. The joy that God gives is greater than the joy of having plenty to eat and drink. It is a joy that lasts.

How may we have this great joy that God longs to give us?

By coming to God as a repentant sinner and receiving His forgiveness and cleansing.

By coming into His presence in prayer — coming to God and telling Him all our problems and bringing our burdens to Him.

By allowing Him to have first place in our lives — letting Him fill our thoughts and our lives with His life.

As we daily open ourselves to God and seek to offer Him the sacrifice of obedience and praise: as we trust Him and live for Him, we shall know the light of His face shining on us and shall experience His joy rising up in our hearts. Because we know His joy and that His face is shining on us we shall have peace and be able to rest in the Lord.

*The LORD has heard my cry for mercy; the LORD accepts my prayer.   Ps 6:9.*

When we are unwell and our body is tired and aching, it often affects our spirit and we can feel that God is far away and that He is angry with us or disciplining us in some way. However we feel, we can still tell God about it. We can tell Him about our sickness and ask for His healing. We can tell Him about the anguish of our soul, and that He seems far away and not answering us. We can ask His help — not because we merit it or deserve it, but because of His unfailing love towards us, which we see most clearly in the sufferings of Jesus and His death on the Cross for us.

No matter how worn out we feel, or how many tears we have shed, whether tears of sadness, or tears of self-pity or frustration, God still loves us, and we can be sure that He has heard our weeping, and that in His own time He will deliver us.

When we feel that everything is against us and that no-one is on our side, we can still call out to God for help, and know that He has heard and has accepted our prayer and will come to our aid.

*When I consider your heavens, the work of your fingers, the moon and the stars, which you have set in place, what is man that you are mindful of him, the son of man that you care for him?   Ps 8:3,4.*

As I was thinking about these words I felt that God was saying to me,

"Yes, My child, look around you,
  Look at the sun, moon and stars.
  I made them all.
  I send the snow and the wind.
  I control all these things.
  Look around and see My Greatness.
  I am the Great and Powerful God,
  And I made man — I made you,
  And I care for you.
  You are My chosen possession and I love you.
  I long for your love in return.
  The sun, moon and stars cannot love Me.
  The earth and the animals cannot love Me.
  I am Love, I desire your love.
  Let your love flow to Me.
  Let your heart be filled with love for Me,
  And I will shower you with the blessings of My love.
  Oh, come to Me, love Me, delight in Me,
  Satisfy My heart with your love."

*The LORD is a refuge for the oppressed, a stronghold in times of trouble. Those who know your name will trust in you, for you, LORD, have never forsaken those who seek you.   Ps 9:9,10.*

Someone told me that she had been going through a difficult time — her daughter went into hospital for an operation, her father was in hospital many miles away, there was something wrong with the car and there were various other problems to face.

Sometimes we go through times in our life when it seems that everything is against us. There can be various reasons for this happening. It may be that we are being oppressed by Satan, or that God is seeking to discipline us because He sees various things in our life that are displeasing to Him, or we may have wandered away from the Lord and He is seeking to stop us in our tracks in order that we may turn back to Him.

Whatever happens to us and for whatever reason, God is watching over us and He sees how we react. Often we resent adverse circumstances and we become angry — with what is happening, with ourselves, and maybe, even with God. But all the time God is reaching out to us, longing for us to seek Him afresh, to trust Him, to seek refuge in Him, to know His presence with us no matter what problems we are facing.

Those who know the name of Jesus — who know that He is their Saviour and Lord — will find that they can trust Him no matter what happens. Whatever our circumstances, may our response be, "I will trust and not be afraid."

*But you, O God, do see trouble and grief; you consider it to take it in hand.    Ps 10:14.*

As I was reading the story of the feeding of the five thousand in John Chapter 6, I was struck by the words, "Jesus already had in mind what he was going to do."

Jesus had asked Philip, "Where shall we buy bread for these people to eat?" and Philip had given an answer, looking at the situation from a practical viewpoint. At times we may feel Jesus is asking us, "What shall we do in this situation, how shall we deal with this trouble and grief?" We try to give some kind of answer, suggesting the use of the resources we have available, which are completely inadequate. Jesus knew the situation which He and the disciples were going to face, even before it happened, and He knew what He was going to do about it.

Jesus knows what troubles and griefs we are going to face, and He knows what He has in mind to do. He is waiting for us to give the whole situation over to Him so that He can do what He already has in mind to do.

*The LORD is in his holy temple; the LORD is on his heavenly throne. He observes the sons of men; his eyes examine them.   Ps 11:4.*

We live in times of increasing violence and wickedness and it seems that the foundations of our society are being destroyed. Sometimes I feel like running away from it all and hiding, but where can I go? Running away from things does not solve the problem. The only person to whom I can go is God because He is my refuge and strength in times of trouble.

God is watching what is going on and He knows about the seeming prosperity of the wicked and the increase of violence. God is Holy and righteous and just, and one day those who deliberately choose to do evil will receive the due punishment for their wickedness, maybe not in this life, but in eternity. We see things from the point of view of our time lived here on earth, but God sees the whole of eternity stretched out before Him. Those who love wicked ways will receive eternal punishment, but those who love God, who know salvation in Jesus and delight in Him, will see Jesus face to face. God is working out His just and righteous purposes, and we can trust Him.

*And the words of the LORD are flawless, like silver refined in a furnace of clay, purified seven times. Ps 12:6.*

There is power in words and they can be used for good or evil. Often they are used to persuade others, and people can be led by the force of a powerful argument. Words can be used to flatter others and to lie in order to achieve one's own ends. Words can wound and hurt and, if we are falsely accused, we seek to defend and justify ourselves. Jesus, before Pilate, remained silent as His accusers hurled words at Him, but we find it hard to remain silent and to allow God to vindicate us.

It is possible for words to distort the truth, and at times, when we hear conflicting reports, we are not sure who or what to believe. One Person whose words we can always trust is God, because He is truth and His words are trustworthy and reliable.

If we are being faced with words and arguments flung at us from all directions and feel weak and in need of help, we can turn to God and trust His Word when He says to us, "Because of the oppression of the weak and the groaning of the needy, I will now arise," says the LORD, "I will protect them from those who malign them." (Ps 12:5.)

*LORD, who may dwell in your sanctuary? Who may live on your holy hill?   Ps 15:1.*

What kind of life does God want His people to live? After we have come to God in repentance and faith, we should seek to live in a way that is pleasing to God. What does this mean in practice? It means that we shall be people who live righteous lives and who seek to be blameless. We shall speak the truth and not pass on gossip nor say unkind things about others. Even if we hear something against someone else, we shall seek to think the best about them at all times. We shall turn away from all that is vile and wicked and shall do all we can to help those who are seeking to promote good and justice. When we make promises to others, we shall keep them, even if afterwards we wish we had not made the promise and even if it means putting ourselves out to keep it. Above all, we shall seek to love others even as God has loved us.

This is indeed a high standard of living, which we cannot attain in our own strength. As we allow God to live in us and as we seek to live in Him and delight ourselves in Him, it can become a glorious reality.

*You have made known to me the path of life; you will fill me with joy in your presence, with eternal pleasures at your right hand. Ps 16:11.*

Some people think that if they have plenty of money, a big house with all the latest gadgets, then they will be happy. Others look for happiness in relationships or having exotic holidays or having plenty to drink. These things may give some happiness and pleasure, but it does not last. It is only God who can give us joy and happiness that is lasting. When we yield ourselves completely to Him and allow Him to run our lives for us, then we shall find Him giving us joy, where we did not expect to find it.

We shall find there is joy and pleasure in being with other Christians and having fellowship with them. We shall find that in humble surroundings and with very little of this world's goods, we can feel secure. We shall find God guiding and directing our life and, even on a sleepless night, we shall know the reality of God's presence with us. We shall find that as we praise God and take delight in Him, He will make us aware of His presence and give us a greater joy that we have ever known before and we shall know that we are safe for time and eternity.

*I have resolved that my mouth will not sin.   Ps 17:3.*

The other day someone said to me that they wished they could take back some of the things that they had said. But once a word is out of our mouths, it cannot be unsaid. Most of us regret some of the things we have said — the angry word which is said in the heat of the moment; the bitter word which has deeply wounded a loved one; the piece of gossip we have passed on, only to find afterwards that it was untrue; the lie we told, which led on to telling more lies.

Yes, at times we do sin with our mouth, and what we say shows what our heart is like. If we are conscious that we are saying wrong and hurtful things and that we are sinning with our mouth, we need to confess this to God and ask Him to give us love for others; to change our heart and our attitude, so that we shall not want to sin with our mouth. And we must also set our mind to say only what is true and loving so that, like Jesus, we may have gracious words coming from our lips.

*In my distress I called to the LORD; I cried to my God for help. From his temple he heard my voice; my cry came before him, into his ears.   Ps 18:6.*

"My child, I hear your every cry for help
  and I will help you.
  I heard your cry this morning.
  Remember how I met with you
  as you read My Word.
  Every time you cry to Me, I hear your cry
  and I will help you.
  The answer may not always be what you expect,
  but I hear and I will deliver you.
  I am the Almighty God.
  There is no one like Me.
  No one has power as I have.
  I am stronger than the strong.
  I overcome all the evil designs of Satan —
  he is already a defeated foe.
  I am the great God and I will lead you out to victory.
  I will give you the strength you need and I will save you.
  Just as I was with my servant David
  and saved him in all his battles
  so I will be with you
  and give you victory."

*He brought me out into a spacious place; he rescued me because he delighted in me.   Ps 18:19.*

"I have delivered you from fear.
I have rescued you from bondage.
I have cleansed you from sin.
I have brought you into a spacious place —
into eternal life in My Son Jesus.
I have rescued you because I delight in you.
I delight in you, My child, and I am glad
when you come to Me.
I delight in your presence, and I am glad
when you trust in Me.
I delight in your love, and I am glad
when you express your love to Me.
I delight in your worship, and I am glad
when you offer Me your praise.
Come to Me, delight yourself in Me.
Satisfy Me with your presence and your love."

*O LORD, the king rejoices in your strength. How great is his joy in the victories you give! You have granted him the desire of his heart and have not withheld the request of his lips. Ps 21:1,2.*

"Believe Me, My child,
 I have already answered your request and have already given you your heart's desire.
 You cannot see it yet, but I am doing those things that you desire.
 There is blessing already, although it cannot yet be seen.
 Do not lose heart,
 Believe that you already have those things which you desire, and you will find that you have them.
 Thank Me for them in advance.
 Do not look on the outward aspect of things.
 You cannot see the deep and hidden work that I am doing.
 Live in the light of My promise.
 Never become discouraged.
 I am with you and will do what I have said.
 I have strength and power.
 I am victorious.
 Rejoice in Me now.
 Thank Me now."

*They cried to you and were saved; in you they trusted and were not disappointed.   Ps 22:5.*

Have you ever felt disappointed with God and imagine that He has let you down? I have. There was a time when I wanted something very much and I prayed and asked God for it, but He did not grant my request. I felt God did not love me and I was very disappointed with God. Now, as I look back, I can see how very selfish I was in what I was asking. I thought that if God gave me what I desired I should be really happy and contented. I realise now that God knew what was best for me and that it was because He loved me that He did not give me my desire.

The times when I have wanted God to fulfil **my** desires and do **my** will are the times when I have felt disappointed with God. The times when I have really sought to do God's will, in spite of what I want or desire, are the times when I have felt true joy. When I have fully trusted God, I have found that I am not disappointed — with God or with what He chooses for me.

*You anoint my head with oil; my cup overflows. Ps 23:5.*

When a full cup gets knocked it spills some of its contents. As we go through life we get knocked and buffeted. I wonder what spills out? When we are knocked by disappointment or buffeted by adversity or upset by others, often it is anger, frustration, unhappiness, self-pity and unkind words which spill out of our life. This is how we behave naturally because we are all born with a sinful nature. Some people have learned to control themselves better than others, but what we all need is a change on the inside, so that these things are not there to spill out. Paul says, "Be transformed by the renewing of your mind." (Rom 12:2.)

David said, "You anoint my head with oil." The head speaks of our mind, thoughts and attitudes, and the oil is often a picture of the Holy Spirit. As we daily ask God to anoint our head with His Holy Spirit and allow Him to renew our mind, we shall find our life being transformed. Then, when we are knocked and buffeted, the gentleness and love and understanding of Jesus will spill out in blessing to others.

"Lord, anoint my head, my mind, my attitudes with the oil of Your Holy Spirit so that the cup of my life will overflow with the life of Jesus."

*Lift up your heads, O you gates; lift them up, you ancient doors, that the King of glory may come in. Who is he, this king of glory? The LORD Almighty — he is the King of glory.   Ps 24:9,10.*

When I first met her, several years ago, she was about 70 years old. She was slightly bent and her face was shrunken and lined. She had been a churchgoer most of her life, but about two years ago, she realised that although she knew about Jesus, she did not know Him in a personal way. She invited Jesus, the King of glory, into her life and He began to comfort her lonely, sad heart. As He did so, she began to stand upright and lift up her head and her face began to fill out and lose many of its lines.

Jesus made a real difference in her life and He can make a difference in our lives, too. As we lift our thoughts up to Him, as we lift our hearts and lives up to Him, Jesus, the King of glory will come in. May we daily lift our hearts and minds up to Jesus that He may come in and fill us with Himself.

*He guides the humble in what is right and teaches them his way.   Ps 25:9.*

A young woman said to me that she did not like other people telling her what to do; she wanted to run her life in her own way. This is true of most of us, even in our Christian life. Often we still want to go our own way and choose what we are going to do and where we intend to go. We make our own plans and then ask God to bless them and we wonder why things go wrong and why we do not find the joy and fulfilment that we expected.

The only way to live the Christian life to the full is to live it God's way, and that means coming to Him in repentance and asking Him to forgive all our sins, including our selfishness, stubbornness and self-will. Then, as we submit ourselves humbly to Him, God will guide and direct our life. May we make the words of David in Psalm 25 verses 4 & 5 our own. "Show me your ways, O LORD, teach me your paths; guide me in your truth and teach me, for you are God my Saviour, and my hope is in you all day long."

*My eyes are ever on the LORD, for only he will release my feet from the snare.   Ps 25:15.*

Imagine walking through a forest where someone has set traps for the animals, and your feet become entangled in one of them. You look down at the snare and try to release your feet, but the more you struggle the worse it becomes.

As we go through life, we become entangled in various problems, and at times we feel that we are in a trap — a snare is holding our feet and we cannot get ourselves out of it. The more we chew over the problem, the more we struggle to become free, the worse it becomes. But, as we turn our eyes away from the problem and look up to the Lord Jesus, we discover Him giving us peace, even while we are still in the trap. As we continue looking steadfastly to Him, we find Him releasing our feet from the snare. Jesus is the only one who can help us and release us from all those things which ensnare us and keep us from living the life of freedom which He won for us by His death on the Cross.

*The LORD is my strength and shield; my heart trusts in him, and I am helped.   Ps 28:7.*

When I was a child, I was told that I must learn to stand on my own two feet and that I must rely on myself. Later on, someone said to me that they thought I was very self-sufficient and that is, no doubt, the appearance that I gave. But underneath I was crying out for love and acceptance. I had tried hard to live a good Christian life but it was all a hard struggle and deep down I knew I was failing God. Because He loved me, God had to bring me right down in order that I might learn to rely on Him and receive His help and strength.

Sometimes God allows us to go through difficult times in order that He may bring us to the end of ourselves — bring us to the place of complete dependence on Him. He longs to show His love for us and to help us, but so often we will not allow Him to. When we admit our weaknesses to Him and ask for His help, we shall find that He is our strength and our shield and that we can trust Him completely.

*You turned my wailing into dancing; you removed my sackcloth and clothed me with joy, that my heart may sing to you and not be silent. O LORD my God, I will give you thanks for ever.    Ps 30:11,12.*

One Saturday morning I woke up feeling out-of-sorts and it turned into one of those mornings when everything seemed to be going wrong. After a while I was near to tears — tears of frustration and self-pity. Then I remembered that God promises to work out things for the good of those who love Him. I started speaking aloud to God, telling Him that I did love Him and that although I did not know why everything seemed to be going wrong, I still trusted Him. Then I began to praise Jesus for His Cross and His great love for me. As I continued to think about God's love, I began to get things back into their right perspective and I realised that my "disasters" of the morning were really not so bad or so important as I had imagined. I had been allowing material things to dominate my horizon, but as I looked beyond them to God, I began to know His joy rising up within me and He gave me a song in my heart.

*I will instruct you and teach you in the way you should go; I will counsel you and watch over you. Ps 32:8.*

When Solomon died, his son Rehoboam became the next king. Rehoboam sought advice from the elders who had served his father and they gave him good advice. But Rehoboam rejected their advice and consulted the young men who had grown up with him. He followed their bad advice and this led to much trouble.

At times we may seek advice from others and sometimes we follow the advice we are given, but it is not always good advice. Perhaps we accept it because we like the person who gave it to us, or because we want to get into their "good books"? Perhaps we follow the advice we are given because what is suggested appeals to us, and we do not stop to consider if it is good or bad advice?

There is one Person who will always give us good advice and that is God. Yet often we do not ask Him about His will for our lives. If we come to God, seeking His will about a matter and we are prepared to follow His advice, then He will guide us and make His will known to us. And since God knows what is best for us, we can be sure that His advice is always good.

*But the eyes of the LORD are on those who fear him, on those whose hope is in his unfailing love. Ps 33:18.*

God is love and because God is also eternal, there is no end and no limit to His love. We are the objects of God's love and He longs that we might know and experience His love. He has given us the light of day so that we can see the wonders of His creation all around us. He has given us the night when we can rest and sleep. He has given us our homes and families and friends.

We may feel that we know very little of God's love, but, if we look around us, we shall see some way in which God's unfailing love is reaching out to us. We grieve God by our sins and our neglect of Him, but that does not stop Him from loving us. We grieve Him by our rebellion against Him and our determination to have our own way, but that does not stop Him from loving us. We make barriers between ourselves and God, but His love is still reaching out to us.

We see His unfailing love most clearly as we look at Jesus on the Cross, dying in our place, paying the penalty of our sin. May we respond to God's unfailing love and put our trust and hope in Him.

*Those who look to him are radiant.   Ps 34:5.*

As I walk along, I sometimes look at people's faces and often I see sad and unhappy faces. In the past people said to me, "Don't look so sad." I looked sad because I felt unhappy, and thought that no-one cared about me or understood me. Over these last few years I have come to know that God, my heavenly Father really does love me; He knows all about me and He cares about what happens to me. He understands me better than I understand myself. As I have sought to get to know God better and have allowed Him to work in my life, He is changing me, giving me a satisfaction in living and a contentment I did not think possible, and something of what He is doing on the inside sometimes shows on the outside because now people have said to me, "It is nice to see your smiling face." What God has done for me, He can do for others. As we look to the Lord, seeking to take delight in Him, and as we allow Him to work in our lives, we can know His joy and love causing us to be radiant.

*The righteous cry out, and the LORD hears them; he delivers them from all their troubles.   Ps 34:17.*

In the Acts of the Apostles we read that when Peter was in prison an angel came and released him from the guard and led him out of the prison. At first Peter thought he was seeing a vision, but after they had walked the length of a street the angel left him, and Peter realised that God had sent the angel to rescue him.

As I read about this incident in my Bible, I was aware that the Lord was seeking to speak to me through it. I had something on my mind, something I was concerned about, and it was as if my thoughts had me imprisoned. I could not get it out of my mind. I prayed, calling out to God, that He would somehow rescue me from the prison of my troubled thoughts.

About two hours later, I had an unexpected phone call and the caller said that he would take care of the situation that concerned me. It was no problem to him and he would deal with it. I felt a burden was lifted from me and I thanked God that He had heard me and had rescued me from the prison of my troubled thoughts.

*They feast on the abundance of your house; you give them drink from your river of delights.     Ps 36:8.*

"Here I am! I stand at the door and knock. If anyone hears my voice and opens the door, I will come in and eat with him, and he with me." (Rev 3:20.)

Jesus is waiting for us to open the door and to invite Him into every area of our life. He wants to come in and eat with us, to share in the ordinary things in our life — to become part of our life. But He desires more than this. He wants us to eat with Him — to share His feast. Jesus is now seated at the right hand of God in the place of power and authority and He longs to share His victorious life with us. Jesus also wants to share with us His love and joy and peace. He wants us to eat with Him — to feast on the abundance of His house and to drink from the river of His delights.

As we allow Jesus not only to eat with us, but to share His feast with us, we shall enjoy rich spiritual blessings. May we delight in the rich feast that Jesus sets before us.

*Be still before the LORD and wait patiently for him.
Ps 37:7.*

"Don't bother me now — I'm busy." "I haven't got time." "I don't know where the time goes these days." I expect these words sound familiar! There never seems to be enough time to do all the things we want to do and sometimes we rush around trying to get everything fitted in and we wear ourselves out in the process. Life is often lived at a hectic pace these days with many pressures on us and some people are unable to take it and become ill as a result.

I am sure God does not want us to live a life of perpetual rush. He wants us to learn to live our lives according to His timing and to wait for Him to show us what to do and what to leave, so that we are not always frantically rushing around.

Just a few minutes alone with God, being quiet in His presence, seeking His guidance, can be a great help in taking away the stress and strain from our lives. I have found verses 1 to 7 of Psalm 37 very helpful. May I suggest that you sit quietly and read them and let God speak to you through them.

*Wait for the LORD and keep his way. He will exalt you to inherit the land.   Ps 37:34.*

The pendulum of the old grandfather clock swung slowly backwards and forwards saying, "Plenty of time, plenty of time." The modern clock on the mantelpiece was ticking furiously saying, "Must hurry, must hurry, must hurry."

Many of us are like the modern clock. Something inside us seems to say, "Must hurry," and we rush around, hurrying from one thing to the next, acquiring as many things for ourselves as we can. We become so concerned with our family, home, clothes, food, car, bank balance, etc., that we have little or no time left over for God. If we put God first, spending time with Him, we shall find that we have time for doing all the things that God wishes us to do.

Let us come to Jesus now, while there is still time, and let Him regulate our lives. May we spend time getting to know Jesus, learning to see Him as He really is, allowing our hearts to go out to Him in love and worship and adoration, delighting in Him, and letting Him exalt us to possess every spiritual blessing in Him.

*He lifted me out of the slimy pit, out of the mud and mire; he set my feet on a rock and gave me a firm place to stand.  Ps 40:2.*

It is a long time since I have crossed a stream on stepping stones. As I was thinking about this, I imagined that there was a crowd of people on one bank and Jesus on the other, calling them one by one to cross the stream.

When we first respond to Jesus and begin our Christian life, it is like stepping off the bank onto the first stepping stone. Then, each time we take a step of faith or obedience, it is like moving onto the next stone. Sometimes, as we move from one stone to the next, our feet slip and we go down into the water. Sometimes in our Christian experience we falter and slip, and the waves of sorrow and sadness, or disappointment or fear seem to come washing right over us. When we call out to the Lord, He lifts us up and puts our feet firmly on the next stone, until at last we reach the other bank.

May we not linger or hesitate, but step out joyfully, and boldly go from one stone to the next, knowing that, He sets my feet on a rock and gives me a firm place to stand.

*Many, O LORD my God, are the wonders you have done. The things you planned for us no-one can recount to you; were I to speak and tell of them, they would be too many to declare.     Ps 40:5.*

"I have plans for you, My child,
   They are plans for good, not for evil.
   My plans are wonderful
   And I am working them out, even now.
   They have been secret plans,
   But now I shall make them known to you.
   As you study My Word
   So I shall gradually unfold My plans.
   It is all there in My Word.
   Read and study My Word.
   Eat My Word — let it sink deep within you.
   As you do this, you will begin to see
   My plans for you unfolding.
   They are many and wonderful.
   Let me show you My plans.
   Let Me work out My plans in your life."

*Why are you downcast, O my soul? Why so disturbed within me? Put your hope in God, for I will yet praise him, my Saviour and my God.   Ps 42:11.*

Do you ever talk to yourself? I do, and I find it a help, especially if I am feeling downcast. Sometimes we feel down for no apparent reason — there is a heaviness and uneasiness within and we do not know why. At such times I find it helps to speak aloud — not really talking to myself, but talking to God — remembering the joy that God has given me in the past, remembering the times of joyful worship with others, the times of delight in God's presence.

When the heaviness comes and all the joy seems a long way away, and even God seems a long way away, it is good to remember the times when we have enjoyed God's presence and the delight He has given us.

When our soul is thirsting for God and we do not know where to find Him, we can tell our soul that this time of darkness will pass. God is our Saviour. He has redeemed us by the blood of Jesus and the time will come when we shall again praise Him and rejoice with others in our worship of God. As we put our hope in God — trust in Him, not in our feelings or circumstances — we can be sure that He will bring us through this time of heaviness and lead us into that place where we shall again praise Him with glad and joyful hearts.

*Then will I go to the altar of God, to God, my joy and my delight. I will praise you with the harp, O God, my God.   Ps 43:4.*

"My child, I know you long for a life that is truly satisfying,
That you want to live the abundant life.
I know you desire joy and that overflowing life.
But do not strive for these things.
Remember that I said that he who loses his life will find it.
Seek Me afresh.
Turn your thoughts to Me.
Let Me be the centre of your whole life.
Let Me fill your whole horizon.
Give yourself to Me as a living sacrifice.
Let Me become your joy and your delight.
I am the source of all true joy.
Come to Me, delight in Me.
Let Me fill you afresh with My life."

*God is our refuge and strength, an ever present help in trouble.   Ps 46:1.*

Imagine a family who are comfortably off and healthy, and all that they do prospers. Then things start to go wrong, and they are faced with various troubles. They say, "Why has God let this happen to us?" When all was well they gave no thought to God, but when things went wrong they blamed Him. Yet even in their trouble God was reaching out to them and wanting them to turn to Him and to know His help and strength.

While all is well and we are prospering, we may ignore God. In spite of this, God loves us, and wants us to know Him and to thank Him for all that He is doing for us and giving us. When trouble comes, God longs for us to reach out to Him and to know Him as our refuge and strength. He is there wanting to help, but instead of asking for His help, we blame Him and still try to manage without Him.

God loves us and wants to take care of us. If we have responded to God and His love while all was well, then, when the troubles come, we shall know that we can turn to Him and experience His help in a very real way.

*Be still, and know that I am God.    Ps 46:10.*

Recently I bought a barometer and I like to look at it to see if the pressure has gone up or down. The pressure changes from day to day, and I know that my feelings go up and down as well. But God does not change. He is always the same reliable God.

As we become still, and get beyond our changeable feelings, we can come to that place where we know God as a living reality. Job did not have an easy time of it, but he was able to say, "I know that my Redeemer lives." Some days we may feel the presence of Jesus and know that He is near us, but on other days He may seem far away. Whether we feel Him or not, we can know that Jesus is alive and that He has redeemed us and freed us from our sins.

Jesus healed a blind man and the man said, "One thing I do know; I was blind but now I see." God longs for us to have that same certainty about what He has done for us so that we can say, "I was blind, but now I see spiritual truths. I did walk in sinful ways, but now I know my sin is forgiven and that I am a child of God."

Let us be still, so that we may experience the reality of knowing God.

*He who sacrifices thank-offerings honours me, and he prepares the way so that I may show him the salvation of God.   Ps 50:23.*

Sometimes, when I am reading the Bible, and thinking about what it means, I find thoughts coming into my mind — sometimes encouraging and sometimes challenging.

God has been challenging me about the need to praise Him and offer Him the sacrifice of praise and thanksgiving. Many times in the Bible we are exhorted to praise God and to rejoice and delight in Him, and I have become conscious of the fact that I do not do this enough.

As I was thinking about this verse, I felt God was saying to me:—

"Why are you so ungrateful?
I have done so much for you.
I even gave My Son and let Him die on the Cross so that you might be forgiven and have eternal life.
I long for you to have a thankful, praising heart.
Give thanks to Me, My child, and you will be surprised at the difference it will make to your whole way of thinking.
Continually give Me thanks, and praise My Name.
Spend time in the secret place, lifting your heart and voice in thanksgiving and praise.
As you do this, I can work in you, bringing about changes in you.
Do not condemn or criticise others.
Keep your eyes on Me and lift your heart to Me, so that I can show you the fulness of My salvation."

*Have mercy on me, O God, have mercy on me, for in you my soul takes refuge. I will take refuge in the shadow of your wings until the disaster has passed. Ps 57:1.*

One of the kings of Israel, Jehoahaz, was troubled by powerful enemies. In 2 Kings 13 verses 4, 5, we read, "Then Jehoahaz sought the LORD's favour, and the LORD listened to him for he saw how severely the king of Aram was oppressing Israel. The LORD provided a deliverer for Israel, and they escaped the power of Aram."

At times we may feel that everyone and everything is against us and that we are being overcome by powerful enemies. At such times, if we seek the Lord's favour, we can be sure that He will listen to us. He sees how severely we are being beset and He has provided a deliverer for us. As we come to Jesus, admitting our weakness and powerlessness to help ourselves, we can know Him helping us, so that we can escape the power of those things which are troubling us. As we seek to take refuge under the shadow of God's wings — as we abide in His presence, we can know His shelter and His protection.

*God has spoken from his sanctuary.   Ps 60:6.*

Our God is a God who speaks. In the Old Testament, we read of God speaking to His people and making His power and His will known to them. The idols which the people made and worshipped had mouths, but they could not speak; they had eyes but could not see; they had ears but could not hear. The One true God is a God who sees and hears and speaks.

At times we may feel that God is far away, that He is cold and silent, like the idols of old, but, if we are willing to come into the sanctuary and quietly wait for Him, He will speak to us in the quiet of our own heart.

God is at work in our world; He is at work in our circumstances. At times we may feel He is doing nothing, and even that He is incapable of doing anything because we are only looking at our own particular situation. As we allow God to give us a wider view, we shall see that He is working out His purposes. He is the One who will help us against the enemy — Satan — who seeks to make us doubt God. When we spend time alone with God, in the inner sanctuary of prayer, we can have the assurance that with God we shall gain the victory.

*Hear my cry, O God; listen to my prayer. From the ends of the earth I call to you, I call as my heart grows faint; lead me to the rock that is higher than I. Ps 61:1,2.*

The first time I visited Amy I thought how dark her flat seemed, and I was conscious of the noise of the traffic from the busy main road outside.

She had been a widow for about five years and missed the love and support of her husband.

The time came when she faced various problems and was finding it more and more difficult to cope with life, or make any kind of decision. Amy's doctor decided that she was in need of treatment and so she went into hospital. With the help of treatment, and the prayers of her friends, Amy began to recover. The time came when she was well enough to return home. Amy did not want to go back to her flat. Arrangements were made for her to move into a modern block of flats where there was a Warden.

When I visited Amy there, I thought what a lovely, bright flat. It was just right for a person on their own. What impressed me most was that Amy's faith in God had grown. She had come to know something more of God's love for her. In her distress she had called out to God and He had met with her. Amy knows from experience that God hears the cry of the needy and that He answers them.

*Trust in him at all times, O people; pour out your hearts to him, for God is our refuge.   Ps 62:8.*

When I am faced with a problem, I find it is helpful to pour out my heart to God — to tell Him all about it. Then I sometimes turn to the Psalms to find help and comfort. One day, when I was doing this, I was aware of God answering me.
"Trust Me, for I will not fail you.
  I keep My promises, many though they be.
  Not one of them will fail — I keep My word.
  Do not worry about anything.
  I have said I will guide you and I will.
  I have said I will show you the path of life and I will.
  Trust Me. Oh, trust Me.
  Do not trust yourself or your own understanding of the situation.
  I can see it all, and I know best."

*May the peoples praise you, O God; may all the peoples praise you. Then the land will yield its harvest, and God, our God will bless us.    Ps 67:5,6.*

A long time ago now, as I was looking at this Psalm, I realised that if people really praised God, then there would be a response from God — the land would yield its harvest and God would bless His people.

Recently I have been thinking about this again and the importance of praising God. At times we may thank God for His goodness to us, but we do not often go on to praise Him for who He is. He is the great Creator, He is the One who causes the crops to grow, He is the One who brings salvation to His people.

If we, as a nation, were to turn to God again and give Him the praise due to His Name, we should begin to prosper and know God's blessing on us as a country. Also, when as individuals, we turn to God and offer Him true praise from our hearts, we shall know God providing for our material and our spiritual needs, and we shall experience God's graciousness to us and know the delight of His face shining on us and His blessing resting on us.

*Since my youth, O God, you have taught me, and to this day I declare your marvellous deeds.   Ps 71:17.*

One September day, when I was a teenager, I walked to school as usual. After school, I caught a bus to a destination a few miles away — we had moved house. That led to a change of church, and I began to attend Bible Class on Sunday afternoons.

One weekend, I went to camp with other members of the Bible Class. On the Sunday afternoon, some of them told how Jesus had helped them in very ordinary situations. For the first time I realised that Jesus was alive and was a real person whom I could know. I asked Jesus to come into my life to be my friend. As I continued to attend the Bible Class, I learnt that Jesus had died on the Cross to pay the penalty for my sins. Because of His death, I could be forgiven. I thanked Jesus for being my Saviour, and asked Him to be Lord of my life. That was the beginning of a relationship which has lasted over the years.

I have moved house several times since those teenage years. I have faced other changes, too, but Jesus has remained a faithful friend and Saviour. The grey hairs are increasing, and sometimes I wonder what the future holds, what other changes I may face. The fact that Jesus has helped me over the years gives me confidence to go on trusting Him. I praise Him for all His goodness to me, and delight in His presence with me day by day.

*Praise be to his glorious name for ever; may the whole earth be filled with his glory. Amen and Amen. Ps 72:19.*

"Praise My Name, for My Name is glorious.
  Praise My Name because it is great.
  My Name is El-Shaddai, I am God Almighty.
  I am the God of power and might.
  I am enthroned over all things.
  My Name is Yahweh — I AM.
  I am the eternal God.
  I always have been and I always will be.
  I do not change. I have no beginning and no end.
  My Name is Immanuel. I am the God who is with you.
  I am not a God who is far off, but I am the ever present God.
  My Name is Saviour. I save My people from their sins.
  I died for you. I bore the penalty of your sins.
  I gave My life for you that you might live —
  that you might know My resurrection life in you.
  My Name is Jesus. I am the Alpha and the Omega.
  I am the beginning and the end.
  Praise My Name now and for evermore."

*My flesh and my heart may fail, but God is the strength of my heart and my portion for ever. Ps 73:26.*

"My child, I will strengthen your heart and I will hold you by your right hand, so that you will be strong and steady.
Many storms will come, but I will strengthen your heart, so that you need not fear.
Remain pure and clean. Keep close to Me. Let no sin separate us.
Then, even when storms and tempests rage around you, your heart will be strong and steadfast.
I long for you to rejoice in Me, even when all around there is trouble and distress, even when things seem to go from bad to worse.
I am the powerful God. Is anything too hard for Me?
Keep looking at Me, trusting Me, praising Me.
I am your joy and your portion for ever."

*I will remember the deeds of the LORD; yes, I will remember your miracles of long ago. I will meditate on all your works and consider all your mighty deeds. Ps 77:11,12.*

I was feeling very down — everything seemed to be going wrong and things were getting worse instead of better. In my distress I turned to the Psalms and the words of Psalm 77 spoke to my heart. Like the Psalmist, I was crying out to God for help. I too, felt that God had rejected me and that He had failed to keep His promises to me.

After he had complained to God, the Psalmist turned his thoughts to what God had done in the past and he remembered how God had worked great miracles for His people. I followed his example, and by an act of the will, I turned my thoughts to the Lord — to Jesus and His wonderful life, His death on the Cross for me, and His resurrection. I remembered that the same power that raised Jesus from the dead is available for us today — available for me. Then I thought about what God had done in my life and His goodness to me. He had seen me through difficult times before, and I knew He would see me through this present crisis. I reaffirmed my faith in God and said with feeling, "Your ways, O God, are holy. What god is so great as our God? You are the God who performs miracles; you display your power among the peoples." (Ps 77:13,14.)

*For the LORD God is a sun and shield; the LORD bestows favour and honour; no good thing does he withhold from those whose walk is blameless. Ps 84:11.*

"My child, I long to bestow blessings on you.
 I desire to give you the fulness of My blessings.
 But your pride, your stubborn pride is in the way.
 Humble yourself. Submit to Me and My chastening.
 Be willing to be nothing —
 absolutely nothing in the eyes of the world.
 When you are truly humble and completely obedient
 to My will, then I will exalt you.
 When your walk is blameless before Me,
 then I will give you the fulness of blessing that you desire.
 The way will be hard.
 Self fights strongly against My Spirit.
 Sacrifice pride on My altar.
 Become a fool for My sake,
 then I will open the windows of heaven and pour out an abundance of My blessings."

*For you, O LORD, have helped me and comforted me.  Ps 86:17.*

About midday, the phone rang. It was my brother. I wondered why he was making a long-distance call during the day, and not waiting until the evening. He told me that Dad had died. It was a shock, but not completely unexpected. Dad had recently celebrated his 88th birthday and had had heart trouble for many years.

Over the years my parents had their ups and downs. They both believed in God and went to church regularly. Several years ago my mother became ill, and Dad cared for her. I could see their faith and trust in God growing and deepening. I saw how the Lord helped Dad at the time of my mother's death.

I knew that I would miss Dad, and I shed some tears. As I was trying to take in the fact that my father had died, the Lord gave me a wonderful assurance that Dad was now rejoicing in heaven. That was a help and comfort to me.

Paul, writing to the Christians at Thessalonica said, "We do not want you to be ignorant about those who fall asleep, or to grieve like the rest of men, who have no hope. We believe that Jesus died and rose again and so we believe that God will bring with Jesus those who have fallen asleep in him."

*O LORD God Almighty, who is like you? The heavens are yours, and yours also the earth; you founded the world and all that is in it.   Ps 89:8,11.*

As we look at our world, we can see many things that speak to us of God, if only we have eyes to see them. As we look at the sky and the stars, all in their appointed places, we see something of the glory and greatness of God and that He is a God of order. As we look at the earth with its vegetation and animals, we see God's provision for His creatures, and we can come to see Him as the God who will supply our needs. As we look at the sea and the rivers and streams, they speak to us of God's great power and also tell us He is the One who can quench our spiritual thirst. As we see new life springing up out of what appears to be dead, we can know that God is the giver of life and that through Jesus His Son, we can experience the reality of new life. All around us are things that speak to us about God, His power, His provision, His love and His life.

"Blessed are those who have learned to acclaim you, who walk in the light of your presence, O LORD. They rejoice in your name all day long; they exult in your righteousness." (Ps 89:15,16.)

*If you make the Most High your dwelling — even the LORD, who is my refuge — then no harm will befall you, no disaster will come near your tent. Ps 91:9,10.*

Where do you live? In a house or flat, perhaps. But where do you live in your thoughts? Do you dwell on sad and unhappy thoughts with regrets and bitterness? It is very easy to dwell with the wrong kind of thoughts, which can cause harm, not only in our mind, but in our body as well.

If we seek to make the Most High our dwelling — if we seek to think about God and to have our mind filled with Him and His love and goodness to us, He will protect us. No harm will befall us — that is, none of the troubles which we face day by day will have the power to harm our mind or body. We shall be able to pass through them, kept safe by God. No disaster will come near the place where we live because God is watching over us and is in control of what happens to us. He will use what we may call disasters to bring us blessing. If we love God and acknowledge that He is Lord, He will look after us.

"Because he loves me," says the LORD, "I will rescue him; I will protect him, for he acknowledges my name." (Ps 91:14.)

*Serve the LORD with gladness; come before him with joyful songs.  Ps 100:2.*

"My child, I made you and you are special and precious to Me.
I have work for you to do, if you will submit fully to Me.
Do not be afraid of serving Me.
Do not hold back.
Serve Me with a glad and joyful heart.
When you yield all to Me and allow Me to use you, you will find that service will bring you joy and delight.
When you yield yourself to Me, for Me to use you, you will find that you will enjoy doing the things I have planned for you to do.
Serving Me will bring you pleasure.
I cannot impress on you enough that you will delight in the service I have chosen for you.
Do not hold back, but gladly yield yourself to Me, and I will use you in ways which you cannot now imagine, ways that will excite you, ways that will leave you breathless with joy."

*You will arise and have compassion on Zion, for it is time to show favour to her; the appointed time has come. Ps 102:13.*

When a person is mourning the death of a loved one, grieving over a wayward child or troubled by a painful situation, it affects their whole being. Often there are many tears, loss of appetite, sleepless nights and their whole body suffers, joining with their spirit in their grief. When they cry out to God out of their loneliness, desperation and helplessness, God hears them and has compassion on them. He comes to them and shows them His special favour and love.

It seems that we often have to come to that place of being at the end of ourselves before we reach the appointed time when God comes to us and shows us His favour. It is good to remember that, although people come and go, situations change, and nothing on this earth is truly permanent, God remains the same. He is always reaching out to us with His love and compassion, wanting to work in our lives in order that the life of Jesus may be seen in us. As we acknowledge the sovereign power of God, He will come to us and He will rebuild our shattered life and the touch of His glory will be seen on us.

*For as high as the heavens are above the earth, so great is his love for those who fear him; as far as the east is from the west, so far has he removed our transgressions from us.  Ps 103:11,12.*

I was talking with a friend who felt that because she had done things that were wrong in God's sight, one day God would punish her for them. Although she had repented and accepted Jesus as her Saviour, she still felt that she deserved punishment.

We know that wrongdoing deserves punishment and we feel that we should receive the punishment for our sins. We find it hard to realise that when Jesus died on the Cross, He bore the punishment for our sins, and that God will not punish the repentant person as well. We may have to live with the consequences of our sin, but that is a different matter.

When we confess our sins to God, He is faithful and just and will forgive our sins. Even when we know that we are forgiven by God, we may still find it hard to forgive ourselves. We still remember the terrible things we have done and do not see how we can possibly escape our punishment.

God in His love and mercy does not hold the sins we have confessed against us. Once we have repented and confessed our sins, then, as far as God is concerned, it is over and done with — removed from His sight, and we are free to walk in newness of life with Him. May we accept the love He offers us in His forgiveness, and then forgive ourselves.

*But at your rebuke the waters fled, at the sound of your thunder they took to flight; they flowed over the mountains, they went down into the valleys, to the place you assigned for them. You set a boundary they cannot cross; never again will they cover the earth. Ps 104:7-9.*

I was very conscious that I had a wrong attitude towards certain circumstances, and I knew that I needed to change this attitude, but seemed unable to do so. As I read the above words, I was aware of God giving me the answer to this problem. I prayed, "Lord, please rebuke this wrong attitude so that at the sound of Your voice it will flee, may it go out of my life, down into the place You have assigned for it. Then, please set a boundary that it cannot cross, so that it will never again have a hold over my mind. Please pour into my life the water of Your Holy Spirit so that I may have the mind of Christ with regard to this situation."

Then I pictured the Lord rebuking the wrong attitude and saw it going out of my life. The Lord shut the door on it so that it could not return. Then I thanked Him that it was done and that He was filling my mind with right attitudes and thoughts. Since then I am aware that my attitude is changing. At times the devil tries to bring back the wrong thoughts, but I tell him that the Lord has dealt with this for me.

I have since prayed in a similar way over other wrong attitudes, and I praise God for the power of His Word and that as He rebukes wrong thoughts and attitudes they do indeed flee. If we ask the Lord to fill each area with His Holy Spirit, He will do so.

*They asked, and he brought them quail and satisfied them with the bread of heaven.   Ps 105:40.*

God led the people of Israel out of Egypt and He guided and protected them. When they were hungry and asked for food, He provided it for them.

Are you hungry for spiritual food and are you looking for real satisfaction in life? If so, then ask God to feed you with the bread of heaven. James says, "You do not have, because you do not ask God." (James 4:2.) Jesus said, "Ask and it will be given to you; seek and you will find; knock and the door will be opened to you." (Luke 11:9.) If we come to God and ask Him to provide us with spiritual food, He will bring us into a deeper relationship with Jesus, because Jesus is the bread of life. As we feed on Jesus, we shall know a deep inner satisfaction, because we shall be receiving life, the very life of Jesus into our life. Ask and you will receive. Ask God to feed you with the bread of life, and you will discover life that is life indeed.

*He opened the rock and water gushed out; like a river it flowed in the desert.   Ps 105:41.*

As I read these words, I was reminded of the words of Jesus, "Whoever believes in me, as the Scripture has said, streams of living water will flow from within him." (John 7:38.) Are there streams of living water flowing from us? Jesus was talking about the Holy Spirit. Is the Holy Spirit flowing out of us into the desert around us? All around are people whose lives are dry and barren and they need the water of the Holy Spirit to bring them life. But no water is flowing from us because we are often hard like a rock. We say we believe in Jesus, but it makes no difference to our hardness of heart towards those around us. As we admit our hardness and coldness to Jesus and ask Him to open our life and our heart so that He can fill us with His Holy Spirit, the streams will begin to flow. As we continue to allow Jesus to fill us with the Holy Spirit, He will be able to open us more and more so that the water of the Holy Spirit will begin to flow out of us in love to others.

May we let Jesus open our heart so that the water of life and love and power will begin to flow and become like a river flowing out into the desert, bringing life to those around us.

*Let them know that it is your hand, that you, O LORD, have done it.   Ps 109:27.*

I went to visit a friend who had been unwell. We chatted for a while, then we had a time of prayer together. As I prayed for her, I held her hands and we both became aware of the presence of Jesus. It was a precious time.

As Jesus travelled around, exercising His healing ministry, He often touched people, and His touch can still bring healing today. The hands Jesus now uses are our hands. The touch of a hand can convey understanding and sympathy, and an arm around the shoulders can bring comfort and strength. But the touch of Jesus through our hands can do more than this — it can bring healing and wholeness. As we not only pray with others, but actually touch them when we pray — whether it be a hand on their hand or the 'laying on of hands', love and the healing power of Jesus can flow from one to the other. May we not isolate ourselves, or insulate ourselves from others, but be prepared to touch them, seeking to bring the healing power of Jesus to them. May we know the joy and delight of Jesus using our hands in such a way that we shall know that it is the Lord who has done it.

*Great are the works of the LORD; they are pondered by all who delight in them.   Ps 111:2.*

"I am the Lord Almighty.
 I am glorious and majestic.
 Look at the vastness of My creation.
 Look at the tiny flowers and insects.
 Ponder the scope of My creation.
 I am gracious and compassionate.
 I see man in his sin,
 I see his lost state.
 In My love, I reach out to him.
 In My love I sent My Son Jesus to rescue him.
 I made a new covenant with mankind through the blood of My Son.
 I do not change,
 I am steadfast, I am faithful.
 There is a way for mankind to come to Me.
 My covenant of redemption still stands.
 Blessed are those who come to Me through the way I have chosen — through My Son Jesus.
 Blessed are those who believe what I say.
 Blessed are those who ponder these things and who live by them."

*He will have no fear of bad news; his heart is steadfast, trusting in the LORD. Ps 112:7.*

Are you afraid of bad news? Afraid of what the doctor might say; afraid that a loved one is dying; afraid that the telephone might ring or a letter come bearing bad news?

Well, there is good news — you need not fear the bad news. How is this possible? If our heart is open to God and if we have a right attitude to Him, then it is wonderfully possible.

If we believe that God is Almighty and all-knowing, and that nothing takes Him by surprise; if we have a right relationship with God and hold Him in reverence and awe, then our heart will be steadfast, stayed upon God.

If we delight in God's Word, and see how He has worked in the lives of others; if we believe His promises, that He is working all things out for our good, we shall find that God is trustworthy.

If we are seeking to live life in obedience to God, then although the times of darkness come, we shall know His presence in them. "Even in darkness light dawns for the upright." (Ps 112:4.)

*For great is his love towards us, and the faithfulness of the LORD endures for ever. Praise the LORD. Ps 117:2.*

"My love for you is great.
 My love is mighty and powerful.
 There is no end to My love.
 In My faithfulness I shall always love you.
 I stretched out My arms on the Cross —
 I laid down My life for you.
 My arms are reaching out still —
 Reaching out in love to you,
 Longing that you may respond to My love.
 I long to hear you tell Me that you love Me.
 When did you last whisper words of love to Me?
 When did you last open your heart in love to Me?
 I desire your love.
 I desire that you tell Me of your love.
 When did you last become excited about My love for you?
 When did you last respond to My love?
 When did you last praise Me with a heart overflowing with love for Me?
 Why is your heart so cold and unresponsive?
 I love you, My child.
 Let Me touch your heart, your mind, your life with My love."

*All the nations surround me, but in the name of the LORD I cut them off. They surrounded me on every side, but in the name of the LORD I cut them off. They swarmed around me like bees, but they died out as quickly as burning thorns; in the name of the LORD I cut them off. Ps 118:10-12.*

As we seek to go on in the Christian life, we may be shocked and even horrified by the wrong thoughts that enter our mind. Even when we are praying, the most awful thoughts can come into our mind and we begin to wonder if we really belong to God at all.

If we have been born again and are filled with the Holy Spirit, where do all these dark and bitter, and self-accusing thoughts come from? We need to recognise that they come from the devil, who will try any trick to spoil our walk with the Lord.

When these evil thoughts come to us, we should cut them off in the name of the Lord. We may feel that they are surrounding us on every side, but we must not entertain them, or turn them over in our mind, but straight away cut them off. When we recognise that they are from the devil and cut them off in the name of the Lord, they will die out.

"Resist the devil, and he will flee from you." (James 4:7.) Once we recognise where these evil thoughts come from and cut them off, we shall find that the devil will flee from us. We need to fill our mind with thoughts of Jesus, acknowledging that He is our Saviour and that He is the One who helps us. On the Cross Jesus won the victory over the devil, and so we can join with the Psalmist in saying, "The LORD is my strength and my song; he has become my salvation." (Ps 118:14.)

*Open for me the gates of righteousness; I will enter and give thanks to the LORD.    Ps 118:19.*

When Jesus died on the Cross, He opened wide the gate of righteousness, because He bore the punishment for our sins. He made it possible for us to come to God and receive His righteousness. When we have entered through that gate and received forgiveness, our response should be one of giving thanks to God. God has answered our cry for mercy. He has forgiven us, cleansed us, clothed us in Christ's righteousness — He has indeed become our salvation. He has made His light to shine on us and brought us out of our darkness into His marvellous light. Each new day should be a day of gladness and rejoicing because of all that God has done for us. He is always with us to help and strengthen us. We need not be afraid of what other people do to us or say about us. God will help us to triumph over all wrong thoughts and attitudes and to cut off from our lives all that is impure and unholy.

The Christian life should be a life of victory and joy and thanksgiving. Jesus has opened the gate through which we may enter right into the very presence of God. Let us join in the festal procession of all who are rejoicing and delighting in God and go right into the very presence of God, taking our thanksgiving with us.

*My soul is weary with sorrow; strengthen me according to your word.   Ps 119:28.*

"Lord, my soul is weary with sorrow, sorrow over my failure to keep Your laws, sorrow over my lack of discipline, my lack of faith and trust in You. Lord, because of the sorrow of my soul, my body too, is weary and my mind is tired.

"Many times in Your Word You speak about giving strength to the weak. You say that, those who hope in the Lord will renew their strength. Lord, may I have that kind of hope in You, complete trust in You and assurance that You are the God of the impossible. As I learn to hope in You, may I know the reality of Your renewing my strength.

"Your Word says, 'But the Lord is faithful, and he will strengthen and protect you from the evil one.' Lord, may I really believe You are the faithful God and that You will indeed strengthen me. May I know Your protection from the evil one as he seeks to plant all kinds of wrong thoughts in my mind. You are the faithful God. Strengthen me according to Your Word.

"You said to Paul, 'My grace is sufficient for you, for my power is made perfect in weakness.' Lord, thank You for Your grace, thank You that Your grace is sufficient for my every need. Thank You that Your power is made perfect in my weakness. Thank You that when I acknowledge my weakness and powerlessness, You come to me with Your strength and I can know and delight in Your strength. Thank You, Lord."

*I run in the path of your commands, for you have set my heart free.  Ps 119:32.*

When we put our trust in Jesus and confess our sins to Him, He forgives our sins and sets our heart free. We need no longer feel bound by past sin and failure because Jesus has given us a new life, a new beginning.

Although Jesus has set our heart free, often we soon become bound again, because we still want to go our own way and follow our own selfish desires. If we want to maintain our freedom of heart we must run in the path of God's commands. A train runs on a track and the track keeps the train going in the right direction so that it will reach the correct destination. We must not think of God's commands as obstacles which stop us from doing what we want, but as tracks that keep us going in the right direction so that we shall reach the correct destination. As we live according to God's rules and take delight in following His principles, we shall not only have our heart set free, but we shall be able to walk about in freedom. "So if the Son sets you free, you will be free indeed." (Jn 8:36.)

*In the night I remember your name, O LORD. Ps 119:55.*

Sometimes I do not sleep very well. I used to worry about it and, of course, the more I worried, the more difficult it was to sleep. I began to realise that, at night, when all is quiet, I can spend time talking with God. Often our days are busy and we are unaware of God because our mind is so full of other things. At night, we can be relaxed and enjoy God's presence.

Sometimes, when I am finding it difficult to sleep, I just start to think about Jesus and say His name to myself and delight in the beauty and power of His name. At other times, I ask the Lord to show me if there is someone in particular for whom He wishes me to pray, or I think about His promises and thank Him for His faithfulness. Sometimes I praise God, using the new prayer language He has given me.

I remember especially one morning when I awoke very early. I started to think about Jesus and His love and to thank Him for all His goodness to me. As I did this, I became aware of God's love in a very wonderful way. Sleepless nights can be a real blessing as we seek to turn our thoughts to the Lord, remembering His name, and what He has done for us.

*Before I was afflicted I went astray, but now I obey your word. It was good for me to be afflicted so that I might learn your decrees. Ps 119:67,71.*

Do we learn from our mistakes and the troubles that come to us? If we do, then we can say, like the Psalmist, "It was good for me to be afflicted." Often we resent the problems, difficulties and hardships that confront us as we go through life and we become bitter about them. But God has a reason for allowing them to come. Perhaps in some way we are straying from God, or are living in disobedience to His laws, and He has brought affliction into our life in order that we may see where we have gone wrong and turn back to Him. The affliction itself may be very painful, but if we use it aright and seek God through it, afterwards, when we look back, we shall be able to say to God, "You are good, and what you do is good."

God longs for us to walk the joyful path of obedience to Him, and when we stray, sometimes the only way to see our error is through affliction. Whatever our present affliction, let us use it to come back to God, and through it learn to live in obedience to His Word and to delight in His law.

*May they who fear you rejoice when they see me. May those who fear you turn to me.   Ps 119:74,79.*

"Lord, may I be a source of joy to my fellow Christians, so that when they see me, they will rejoice. May I not have a sad countenance or a downcast spirit, but may I so delight in You, Lord, that Your joy will shine out of my face and touch my whole life, so that I will radiate Your joy to others.

"Lord, may I be so filled with the love and compassion of Jesus that those of Your children who have troubles and burdens will turn to me and find a listening ear and sympathetic heart. May I so know Your unfailing love comforting me, and Your compassion coming to me in my times of trouble, that I shall be able to understand others and comfort them in their time of need."

"Praise be to the God and Father of our Lord Jesus Christ, the Father of compassion and the God of all comfort, who comforts us in all our troubles, so that we can comfort those in any trouble with the comfort we ourselves have received from God." (2 Cor 1:3-5.)

*I have not departed from your laws, for you yourself have taught me.   Ps 119:102.*

After I had been married a few months, I went to help with a girls' camp for a week. I can remember waiting for a letter from my husband and when it came, I eagerly read and reread it. In it he told me what he had been doing and he also assured me of his love for me and told me that he missed me.

In a sense the Bible is God's letter to us. It is His Word to us, His voice speaking to us. He wants to communicate with us, to tell us what He is like, what He has done and to assure us of His love for us. He is eager to speak to us and yet we spend so little time listening to Him. He has many things to say to us and He wants us to spend time reading and rereading His Word — listening to what He wants to say to us.

If we spend time reading the Bible — praying that we may recognise God's voice and expecting Him to communicate with us, the Bible will begin to come alive to us in a new way, and we shall find that God is speaking through it. If we let God teach us through His Word and seek to live in obedience to that Word, we shall find great joy and delight in our times of Bible reading.

*Make your face shine upon your servant. Ps 119:135.*

I enjoy sitting in the sun. As I feel the warmth of the sun on my body, I begin to relax. As I soak up the warmth from the sun, a sense of wellbeing and contentment begins to flow over me.

I long to see God's face shining on me more and more; to enjoy the warmth of His presence; to experience His sunlight dispelling the mists of doubt and fear and gloom; to know that, as His servant, what I am doing is pleasing to Him. I want to delight in the sunlight of His face shining on me so that I may know God giving me that sense of wellbeing and contentment; to be able to say with Paul, "I have learned to be content whatever the circumstances."

"Father, whatever the weather — hot or cold, wet or dry, sunny or cloudy, whatever my circumstances — easy or difficult, smooth or rough, happy or sad, please may I rejoice that Your face is shining on me, Your servant."

*I lift up my eyes to the hills — where does my help come from? My help comes from the LORD, the Maker of heaven and earth.   Ps 121:1,2.*

How often do we lift our eyes to the hills and remember that God made them, and receive encouragement from the fact that He made heaven and earth? How often are we still and silent before our Creator? More often we rush from one thing to the next, and when we sit, our minds are still active. We make plans, or go over some problem, or we turn on the TV or radio. God longs for us to have times when we cease from our activity to be alone with Him. He wants us to get to know Him, to delight in Him, to know something of the splendour of His majesty and the power of His might. He is reaching out to us in many ways, but often we are too busy to notice.

Perhaps for a moment we feel elated by a lovely view or moved by a beautiful flower, but we quickly move on, without realising that in that moment God wanted to meet with us and to know that our hearts were responding to Him. We are so busy that often we are not aware of His presence. Yet God is there, seeking to make Himself known to us through the things He has made. God is seeking to remind us of His power and might by the wonder of His creation, in order that we may turn to Him and find our help in Him.

*The LORD will keep you from all harm — he will watch over your life; the LORD will watch over your coming and going both now and for evermore. Ps 121:7,8.*

Years ago, so I have heard, a wealthy merchant was travelling through dangerous country. At night as he and his companions made camp, some robbers drew near. They were surprised to see high walls all round the camp and no way in. The next day they secretly followed the merchant and that night again there were walls around the camp. On the third night they found gaps in the walls and crept into the camp. The leader of the robbers was puzzled and afraid but found the merchant and said that if he would explain about the walls, he would come to no harm.

After some thought, the merchant realised the meaning of the walls and told the robber that every evening he prayed for himself and those with him, asking God to keep them safe. But that night he had been tired and sleepy and was half-hearted about his prayer, and so the wall of protection was incomplete. As we commit ourselves and those we love to God we can know His wall of protection built around us.

*For the sake of the house of the LORD our God, I will seek your prosperity. Ps 122:9.*

The house of the LORD our God — to David it was the Tabernacle. For us, it is the church which we attend to worship God. I hope that, like David, we rejoice when it is time to go into God's house and that we delight in our worship of God.

The more we pray for the church we attend, the more its worship will be a joy and delight to us. Let us pray for peace — that we may know peace with God because our sins are forgiven through Christ; that we may experience the peace of God guarding our hearts and minds; that there may be peace between us, brothers and sisters in Christ, truly united to Christ and to each other.

Let us pray that we may know the security that comes from loving God and from being accepted and wanted by others. Let us pray that we may have a real desire to see the work of God prosper in His house, so that in our worship there will be a real awareness of God that will bring joy to our hearts. Let us pray that in His house many will find true life in Christ, and experience that peace which transcends understanding.

*We have escaped like a bird out of the fowler's snare; the snare has been broken, and we have escaped. Ps 124:7.*

The devil constantly sets his nets to trap us. Sometimes we are deceived by his wiles and fly around in panic, thinking there is no escape. But, praise God, Jesus has broken the snare so that we can escape and fly up to Him, up to the place of safety. On the Cross, Jesus triumphed over the devil so that none of his traps need hold us, or keep us bound. The devil will try to keep us trapped, caught in our doubts and fears and worries, but, if we look to Jesus and seek His help, He will show us the way out of the trap, so that we can fly unhindered.

Jesus said that He had come to proclaim freedom for the prisoners, and that the truth He proclaimed would set us free. As we realise the truth that the snare is broken because of all that Jesus accomplished by His death and resurrection, we can escape from the devil's traps and fly to Jesus and delight in His liberating power.

*As the mountains surround Jerusalem, so the LORD surrounds his people both now and for evermore. Ps 125:2.*

The king of Aram was at war with Israel, but the prophet Elisha told the king of Israel the plans of the king of Aram so that he was able to avoid capture. This enraged the king of Aram who decided to send men to seize Elisha. It was reported to him that Elisha was in Dothan and so he sent his army to Dothan. They travelled by night and surrounded the city.

In the morning, Elisha's servant went out and he saw the enemy surrounding them. Elisha told him not to be afraid and he prayed that the servant's eyes would be opened. When the servant looked out again he saw the hills full of horses and chariots of fire surrounding Elisha. He saw something of the hosts of God, who far outnumbered the enemy.

Often, like that servant, we see the problems and difficulties surrounding us. We feel afraid and do not know what to do. Whether we see them or not, God's mighty hosts are surrounding His people and God Himself is surrounding us with His love. Oh, that our spiritual eyes might be opened to see that God is surrounding us and that His heavenly army is protecting us, so that we need not tremble or fear. "Those who trust in the LORD are like Mount Zion, which cannot be shaken but endures for ever." (Ps 125:1.)

*Our mouths were filled with laughter, our tongues with songs of joy. Then it was said among the nations, "The LORD has done great things for them." Ps 126:2.*

When God brought the people of Israel back from captivity they were so happy — it seemed too good to be true — that they laughed and sang songs of joy because of all that God had done for them. He had turned their sorrow into joy and they expressed their joy by singing songs of praise to God. Other nations saw the joy of Israel and acknowledged that God had done great things for them.

God is doing great things for us all the time, but so often we do not realise what God is doing. We are sad and walk around with long faces, but if we reach out to God and turn to Him in our sorrow and sadness, He can restore our fortunes and put a song of joy on our lips.

God longs for His people to enjoy Him, to take delight in Him, to rejoice in Him — and when we do, He gives us His joy in our hearts, He puts a smile on our faces and a song of praise on our lips. When others see our joy and delight in the Lord and the difference He is making in our lives, they may come to realise that God has done great things for us.

Jesus said, "Let your light shine before men, that they may see your good deeds and praise your Father in heaven." (Matt 5:16.)

*They have greatly oppressed me from my youth, but they have not gained the victory over me.   Ps 129:2.*

God wants His people to live in victory over sin and all the temptations of the enemy. Paul says, "For sin shall not be your master, because you are not under law, but under grace." (Rom 6:14.)

From our youth we may have had to live in difficult circumstances, aware of evil and bad influences around us, but, as we commit ourselves to the grace of God, we can experience Him giving us the victory, so that wrong things around do not penetrate our lives or cause us to go away from God.

As we go through life trusting in Jesus and His righteousness, we can be filled with His Spirit, so that the pull of wrong desires and evil practices begin to lose their attraction for us. Satan will try to bind us with all kinds of wrong and sinful desires. Jesus came to set the captives free and, as we yield more and more to the desires of His Spirit within us, we shall find Jesus cutting us free from wrong desires within and the temptations around us, so that we no longer desire sinful pleasures, or want to acquire more and more material possessions, or glory in the adulation of others. It becomes possible for us to know the experience of the Psalmist, "But the LORD is righteous; he has cut me free from the cords of the wicked." (Ps 129:4.)

*Out of the depths I cry to you, O LORD; O LORD, hear my voice. Let your ears be attentive to my cry for mercy.   Ps 130:1,2.*

Sometimes God allows us to hit rock bottom because it is only then that we will cry out to Him. When all is going well, we think we can manage our own lives and we go on pleasing ourselves, unaware of the many things in our lives that are displeasing to God.

In order to get our attention, God may lead us through difficulties. Sometimes, even then, we still do not turn to Him and allow Him to work in our lives. Even when we hit rock bottom, we still do not turn to God, but weep with self-pity, or become angry and lash out at others. But all the time, God, in His love, is wanting us to cry out to Him, to admit our need of Him, to ask for His mercy. When we do cry out for mercy, God is able to work in us and show us His love, and also to show us the things in our lives that are displeasing to Him and which are also hurting and harming us and other people. When we begin to see what we are really like, we realise that if God kept a record of our sins, we should be utterly lost. But, praise God, there is forgiveness with Him. If we confess our sins to God, He is faithful and just and will forgive our sins and purify us from all unrighteousness.

We can find forgiveness with God, not because we deserve it, but because Jesus, the sinless Son of God died in our place, bearing the penalty of our sins. Because of Jesus and His shed blood, when we cry out to God, when we cry for mercy, God will hear and forgive us and we shall be able to stand before Him, clothed in Christ's righteousness.

*I wait for the LORD, my soul waits, and in his word I put my hope.   Ps 130:5.*

Some time ago, I sought God about a certain matter and He gave me a verse of Scripture to claim as a promise from Him. As time went by the situation grew worse and I reminded God of His promise to me and He gave me another verse confirming what He had previously said to me. For a time things improved, but later the situation deteriorated and I wondered if God would really do what He had promised.

I know that at times I am impatient. I want God to do things my way and when I want them done. I realise now that during this time of waiting, God is teaching me many valuable lessons and this is not a wasted time. I must continue waiting for Him to work out His promise in His way and in His time. I must continue to hope in His word to me, knowing that God is faithful and that He will do what He has promised. As I wait and keep watch, I know that one day I shall have the delight of receiving from God what He has promised.

*But I have stilled and quieted my soul; like a weaned child with its mother, like a weaned child is my soul within me.   Ps 131:2.*

Like a weaned child with its mother — lying content and at peace in its mother's arms, safe and secure and satisfied — is it like that with our soul — in our inmost being? Is there that stillness and quietness within? When our body aches or we are in pain, is there still that sense of safety and security? When all around is noise, and hustle and bustle, is there still that sense of peace? When there is unrest and turmoil around, do we have that inner sense of God meeting our every need? We have to cultivate this inner composure, to put all negative and agitated thoughts out of our minds and remember that through Jesus we are children of a loving heavenly Father and that we are safe in His arms.

When wrong thoughts assault us, we must resist them and not allow them to enter our minds, because once they have gained access and we think about them, and ponder them, they can sink down into our inner being, upsetting our sense of God's peace and presence. As we fill our minds with thoughts of Jesus and His love, it is wonderfully possible to have that centre of inner peace deep within us, and we can rest in our Father's arms, safe and secure in His love.

*Let us go to his dwelling-place; let us worship at his footstool — arise, O LORD, and come to your resting place, you and the ark of your might. May your priests be clothed with righteousness; may your saints sing for joy. Ps 132:7-9.*

As the Jews went up to Jerusalem to worship God, this is one of the Psalms which they would have sung. They prayed that they might know God's presence in His Temple and sense His power among them, and that they might offer true and joyful worship to Him.

As we go to God's house to worship Him in the company of other believers, I wonder if our thoughts are wandering. Are we thinking about all the things that we want to do, or turning over in our minds things that have happened, or do we pray, even as we make our way to God's house — pray that we may know God's presence and the power of His Spirit among us and that our worship might be pure and holy and joyful?

The Jews prayed and God gave them His answer: "For the LORD has chosen Zion, he has desired it for his dwelling: 'This is my resting place for ever and ever; here I will sit enthroned, for I have desired it — I will bless her with abundant provisions; her poor will I satisfy with food. I will clothe her priests with salvation, and her saints shall ever sing for joy.'" (Ps 132:13-16.) The answer which they received was more wonderful than they could imagine. How gracious God is! If we keep God's commands and seek to walk in His ways, then we too, shall find God answering us as we pray about our times of worship — we shall find God coming to us, as He is enthroned on our praises. We shall see Him blessing us with abundant provisions and satisfying our longing hearts. We shall experience His salvation with such joy in our hearts that we will want to lift our voices in praise to Him continually.

*Lift up your hands in the sanctuary and praise the LORD. Ps 134:2*

In the past the English people have tended to keep their emotions very much to themselves. We have not expressed how we feel except in a very reserved way. Things however, are changing, as anyone who watches sport will realise. People are beginning to show their feelings very positively and vocally.

In the Church in the past we have been so afraid of emotionalism that any display of emotion has been very much discouraged. I am so glad that changes are taking place here too. We usually stand to sing hymns and often anyone looking at us would have the impression that our worship is very cold and unfeeling — a duty rather than a joy. I am pleased that now people are beginning to express their joy and delight in worship by following the Biblical example of raising their hands in praise to the LORD, and clapping their hands to extol Him. The more I seek to praise God, the more I want to express that praise, not just with words, but expressing that praise with my body — reaching out my hands to God as I delight in His presence, opening my hands to Him to receive His blessing. "Lift up your hands to the King of Kings; Praise Him in everything."

*Praise the LORD, for the LORD is good; sing praise to his name, for that is pleasant.   Ps 135:3.*

Many of the Psalms call us to praise God, but at times this is not easy. Perhaps we feel burdened and cast down and think there is nothing for which we can praise God. When we turn our thoughts away from our problems and think about God and His love for us, it is possible to offer praise to Him. As we praise God for Himself, for His love and greatness and power, and as we seek to take delight in Him, we shall find that He will give us His joy, and we shall want to continue praising Him and rejoicing in His presence. Then as we face our problems again, we begin to see them in a different light and realise that as we keep our minds on God, He does help us. God does not change. He is the same loving God who gave His Son for us. As we praise and thank Him for His love and the gift of His Son, we shall find our attitude changing. Instead of being downcast, there will be a song of joy on our lips, given to us by God Himself, and we shall find that it is indeed pleasant to praise the LORD and a delight to sing praise to His Name.

*Give thanks to the LORD, for he is good. His love endures for ever. Ps 136:1.*

We have much for which we can thank God. He is good, and if we have our spiritual eyes open, we shall see many ways in which God is good to us.

I was on holiday and the weather was wonderful. I was aware of God the Creator of this world, being good to me in allowing me to relax in the sunshine in beautiful surroundings.

God is good to us in so many ways, but especially in allowing Jesus to die on the Cross, where He bore away our sins, so that we can be set free from the bondage of our old life. God is watching over us as we move on in our Christian life. He helps us through the difficulties, and if we keep on walking with Him, He will lead us on to the place which He has prepared for us.

God is good; His love endures for ever. Wherever we are, whatever stage we have reached in our Christian life, we can experience the love of God reaching out to us.

Let us give thanks to God, the King of kings and Lord of lords. He is good, His love endures for ever.

*When I called, you answered me; you made me bold and stout-hearted.   Ps 138:3.*

God knows us better than we know ourselves. He knows how weak we are and how often we feel afraid. He knows how much we need His help, and He wants us to come to Him, admitting our areas of weakness so that He can fill them with His strength and power by His Holy Spirit. Often we are afraid of people — afraid of what they will think, afraid of how they will react.

Peter was afraid — afraid of a servant girl and so he denied his Lord. How different he became after he was filled with the Holy Spirit. He stood up before a crowd of people and spoke about Jesus, no longer afraid, but bold and stout-hearted.

God is the same God today. He wants to change us from being afraid to being bold and stout-hearted. Often we are proud and think we can manage without God, but we cannot. As we humble ourselves before God and realise our need of Him and call out to Him, He will answer us.

The Holy Spirit has been poured out, and He is available for us today. If we ask God to fill us with His Spirit and accept by faith the gift of His Spirit, we shall know God's Holy Spirit coming upon us and filling us, making us bold and stout-hearted.

*Though I walk in the midst of trouble, you preserve my life; you stretch out your hand against the anger of my foes, with your right hand you save me. The LORD will fulfil his purpose for me; your love, O LORD, endures for ever — do not abandon the works of your hands.    Ps 138:7,8.*

When we are sorrowing, or in pain, or under attack from the devil, we may think that no-one understands how we feel. People may say comforting words to us to try to help us, but it is possible still to feel that they do not really know what we are experiencing. We may try to explain our problems to them, but their replies to us only enforce the feeling that they are not on our wavelength.

We may feel completely alone in our pain and suffering, and think that everyone is against us, even God. We can be so wrapped up in our own feelings that we doubt the Word of God and His love for us.

Others have walked this lonely path before us, and have found that God does not fail. They have really experienced God's love reaching out to them in their trouble. David of old knew that God was watching over his life, but there were moments of doubt — "Do not abandon the works of your hands," he cried out — but deep down he knew that God's love endures for ever.

Whatever our situation, if we reach out to God, He will respond to us, even although we may not be aware of it at the time. God will stretch out His hand to save us and He will fulfil His purpose for our life.

*O LORD, you have searched me and you know me. You know when I sit and when I rise; you perceive my thoughts from afar.     Ps 139:1,2.*

God knows us and all about us. He saw us before we were even born. God watches over us and, day by day, He sees all that we do. As I was thinking about this and marvelling at God's complete knowledge of me, I felt He was saying to me,
"I know all about you, My daughter,
 I know all your weaknesses,
 I know all your fears,
 But I still love you with an everlasting love.
 I know every move you make,
 I know every thought you think,
 I know everything you plan,
 But I still love you with an everlasting love.
 I know you are Mine,
 I know that I am working out My purposes in you,
 I know that one day you will be with Me, here at My side,
 And I will love you with an eternal, overwhelming love."

*But my eyes are fixed on you, O Sovereign LORD; in you I take refuge — do not give me over to death. Ps 141:8.*

"Keep looking to Me, My child,
  keep your eyes fixed on Me.
  Do not look at the waves,
  do not look at the storm around you,
  or the billows seeking to engulf you.
  Look to Me.
  Keep your eyes on Me.
  Look at My Word.
  Think about My Word.
  Trust My promises.
  The storm will not harm you.
  You are safe while you have your eyes fixed on Me.
  Look into My face,
  look into its fulness,
  and I will meet with you."

*Let the morning bring me word of your unfailing love, for I have put my trust in you. Show me the way I should go, for to you I lift up my soul.   Ps 143:8.*

When I wake in the morning, I thank God for the new day and ask Him that I may be conscious of His love during the day, and that He will guide me and show me what He wants me to do. As I go through the day, I seek to obey the inner promptings of the Holy Spirit, trusting that God is guiding me. Sometimes He graciously lets me know that I am doing the right thing.

One day I kept thinking about a certain friend — I will call her Beryl. I felt concerned about her and decided to write a letter to her. A few days later Beryl phoned and thanked me for writing, and said that the letter had come at just the right time. She had been feeling very down and it was an encouragement to her to receive my letter. In my heart, I thanked God that He had prompted me to write at that time.

On another occasion, I felt that I should visit Ella and when she opened the door to me, she said that she was really pleased to see me, and that I was an answer to her prayer. Ella was facing a problem and wanted to discuss it with someone; I arrived just at the right time.

If daily we commit our life to God, He will show us the way to go and His Spirit will lead us. If we trust God and obey His leading, we shall have the delight of knowing God's unfailing love filling our lives.

*All you have made will praise you, O LORD; your saints will extol you.  Ps 145:10.*

I looked out of the window as the sun was setting and the outline of a tree looked black against the lighter sky behind it. The sun disappeared, leaving lovely golden tints on the clouds. As I watched, the colours changed and it was really beautiful. I stood by the window, thinking about God, the Creator, who has made such lovely colours and variety in nature. I spoke aloud, thanking and praising God for such loveliness and then I began to sing His praise.

I thought that it was a good thing that I was alone and no-one could hear me — yet I was not alone, because I became increasingly aware that God, this wonderful Creator, was with me, and that He was glad that I was praising Him. Such moments can lift us up out of the ordinary things of life and bring us a touch of heaven. Yet they pass all too quickly as we go on our way, continuing with the routine things of life, but their memory can stay with us to encourage us and bring a new quality of life to all that we do.

*The LORD is near to all who call on him, to all who call on him in truth. He fulfils the desires of those who fear him; he hears their cry and saves them. Ps 145:18,19.*

"When you call, I am there; I am near, not far away.
When you are down, or on the mountain top,
I am there. I will not leave you.
I am waiting for you to call to Me and I will answer.
You cannot see Me yet, but I am here, close by your side,
Waiting to satisfy you, waiting to give you your desires,
Waiting for you to call to Me, to tell Me about your longings."

"This is My desire — that you call to Me.
I could give you what you want without your asking.
But I desire that you come to Me, that you call on Me
That you ask Me.
Then I will give — I will give an abundant supply —
More than you asked, more than you expected.
Come to Me, call on Me,
I am near, I will answer."

*The LORD delights in those who fear him, who put their hope in his unfailing love.   Ps 147:11.*

"My child, I do take pleasure in those who fear Me,
  in those who reverence Me, who come before Me
  in adoration and worship,
  in those who hope and trust in My unfailing love."

"It gives Me delight when you spend time with Me,
  when you want to know My presence.
  But do not try to become too familiar with Me."

"Remember, I am the LORD, I am the Holy One.
  I am the exalted God, I am the all-powerful One.
  Come with lowliness, come with awe and wonder,
  and I will take pleasure in you
  and give you delight in My presence."

*He spreads the snow like wool. Ps 147:16.*

Scientists have studied snowflakes under the microscope and have found that they all have different patterns. It amazes me that the great God, who made the whole universe with distances so vast we cannot even imagine them, should trouble to make snowflakes with different patterns. It shows how much God cares about details. He cares about small things as well as big things and is interested in the smallest details. Perhaps if we face a big problem or have to make an important decision, we ask God to help and guide us, but what about small things? Sometimes we think that they are too small to bring to God. God loves each one of us, and is interested in the small details of our lives as well as the big decisions and problems we face.

God, the creator of the universe; God, who is interested in the smallest details of His creation, loves us and cares about every detail of our lives. What a wonderful God He is.

*Let everything that has breath praise the LORD.
Ps 150:6.*

"Praise the LORD, for He is great and mighty.
 He rules over the power of the sea.
 He is mightier than the pounding waves.
 He is stronger than the gale-force winds.
 Yet He is gentle and kind
 like the soft breeze of summer.
 He is more splendid than all the flowers
 arrayed in their summer glory."

"I am weak and feeble, I have no strength,
 but when I think of the LORD and His greatness,
 He lifts me up and carries me along.
 He puts His loving arms around me
 And I am safe and secure."

"I will praise Your Name, I will magnify You, O LORD,
 for You are worthy of all praise and adoration.
 I will delight in Your presence,
 O LORD, my God."